Once Upon A Blue Rock

Laura Dobson

Presentation by *BookLeaf Publishing*

Web: www.bookleafpub.com

E-mail: info@bookleafpub.com

ISBN: 9789357441636

First edition 2023

To my family.

Once Upon A Blue Rock.

Off we went to the point,
Shining sun and briny breeze.
Past the black rocks and the little house,
Scramble over the bank.

Sand worms glisten on the foreshore.
Gulls in the sky, Oyster catchers in the shallows.
What shall we play today.
A car, A plane, A bus.

Any and all considered.
With hopping and jumping, squealing and
shrieking.
Not just your bog standard rock,
All weathered and beaten.

Rough and smooth,
Shiny and cracked
Lichen growing in yellow and green.
A single beach daisy.

Seating more than a few.
Pay the bus conductor with shiny pebbles.
Steering with a stick.
Keep all limbs in the vehicle.

Hours of fun, singing and laughing.
Tides rising and darkening dusk.
Back to granny's we run.

Tomorrow,
We can go back to the big, blue rock.

Tidal

White horses stampeding to the shore.
Pebbles clink and clack, rolling back.
Sea weed sticking to the sand.
Spray whips, droplets splashing
Bubbles breach and swirl.
Current drawing
Pulling back
Tide goes
Out.

Sea Shells

Remnants of Summer;
Under grains of crystal sand
Small conical shell.

The Elephants House

Sharply, turning towards the sky.
Heavy rocks and ditches high.

A hidden world, lies behind the greenery.
Pushing past the shrubbery.

The well worn path, slim and raw.
Follow well, the drop is yaw.

Cottages below, concealed in leaves.
Peeking out our laughter heaves.

Soaring high, the endless view.
Cresting waves and shimmering blue.

Cast a look out between the islands
Uninhibited to foreign lands.

Back along the path at height
Along the river dim with street light.

A look back, up above.
The secret is still safe.

Dark Sky

Ever blackest night.
Autumnal equinox; bleak
Earth spinning fast.

The Dark Sky

The dark sky
Pale blue night
light, the sun came to shine.
To stall the time.

A poem by Tobias Dobson,
Age 8.

Genisis

Volcanic eruptions render the air.
Terra formed and ripe, life ignites.
Warm pools nurture archaea.
Seas teeming, land breathing.
Tree of life imparts.
A world full.
Bright and new.
Explore
Space.

Pebbles

That smooth shiny rock appeals to me,
Pick it up, eager hands feeling.
In my pocket, kept safe.
Out on the shelf, sunlight.
Bringing the sparkles,
A glitter of
Muscovite.
Mica
Schist.

Igneous

Out of the deep,
Pouring, flowing, heat

Cooling, hardening heap.
Time goes by, never missing a beat.

New land to keep
Desires marked out by feet.

White cliffs

Rising up above the sea,
Into the clouds with birds above.
Covered with thin layers of soil and grass,
Sun baked and hard packed.

Millions of lifeforms, plain to see.
What is not to love.
More time will pass.
Brutal waves attacked.

Tectonics

Ever changing,
Never Still.
Deforming, renewing,
Building and converging.

Pushing, pulling.
Collision and subduction.
Continents with oceans
A restructure to come.

Darkness

Out of the darkness,
did the ember burn.
Slowly retreating,
the darkness became
a mistress to the glowing.

Working much deeper,
the darkness eludes
the glory is not for darkness.

Humans

Earth turning,
A world unencumbered.

Just a blink,
That's all it took.

Cyclical nature
The fire and the ice

Hunger and greed
Two sides of the divide

Fire aflame
The ice dwindles.

Soon we will perish

Water

Rivers, streams and burns.
Lochs, lakes and lagoons.
Oceans abound.

Flowing freely, dripping and gushing.
Yet, solid, serene, soft.

Icebergs stately and calving.
Snow pristine and falling.
Rain and hail, pelting and driving.

Trapped in our bodies,
Animals and plants.
Water means survival and home.

Moisture in the atmosphere,
Deep underground.

Salty brine, mineral fresh.
Contaminated and unpotable.
Uniquely Earthbound.

Metamorphism.

Unchanging for millions of years.
Pressure, rising temperatures.
Pushing, folding and squeezing.
Changing in time and space.
Growing crystalline.
On to the new.
Degrees of
Matter.
Gneiss.

First Snow.

Grey nimbostratus,
Threaten snow. Icy cold air
Sucks moisture; Snow drifts.

Flow

From a crack in solid rock,
A trickle flows out.
Down the mountain in to the loch.
A stream continues without doubt.

Gravity, drawing the flow over bedrock.
Wider, wider the river sprouts.
Ripples, eddies and currents swirl around a
dock.
Rushing river firth empties with a clout.

Might river meets ocean, in for a salty shock.
Silt deposits change as tides draw out.
Sand bars alter and move, sea birds squawk.
That little trickle is carried away, then drops out.

Gaia.

At the core our heart.
Summer; plants our lungs transpire.
Biota balance life.

www.ingramcontent.com/pod-product-compliance
Lightning Source LLC
La Vergne TN
LVHW050310200726
843509LV00015B/3265